DIABETIC SMOOTHIE RECIPES FOR BEGINNERS

The Comprehensive Guide for the Newly Diagnosed to Take Control of Diabetes and Lower Blood Sugar Levels With 30 Easy and Tasty Fruit Blends

MICHAEL JAMMY

Copyright © 2024 Michael Jammy

All rights reserved. No part of this book may be reproduced in any form or by any electronic or mechanical means, including information storage and retrieval systems, without written permission from the publisher, except for the inclusion of brief quotations in a review. This book is a work of non-fiction. Any resemblance to actual persons, living or dead, or actual events is purely coincidental. All information has been provided through research, interviews, and/or personal experience.

SCAN TO GAIN ACCESS TO MORE VALUABLE BOOKS FROM ME

TABLE OF CONTENTS

INTRODUCTION 5
Understanding Diabetes: 6
    Types of Diabetes: 6
    Causes: 6
    Importance of Diet in Diabetes Management: 6
    Importance of Smoothies for Diabetes Management: 7
THE 30 EASY AND TASTY RECIPES FOR BEGINNERS 8
    1. Berry Bliss Smoothie - Prep Time: 5 minutes 8
    2. Green Energy Boost Smoothie - Prep Time: 7 minutes 9
    3. Citrus Delight Smoothie - Prep Time: 6 minutes 9
    4. Almond Joy Smoothie - Prep Time: 5 minutes 10
    5. Tropical Paradise Smoothie - Prep Time: 8 minutes 10
    6. Apple Cinnamon Spice Smoothie - Prep Time: 5 minutes 11
    7. Pomegranate Punch Smoothie - Prep Time: 7 minutes 12
    8. Avocado Berry Burst Smoothie - Prep Time: 6 minutes 12
    9. Spinach Pineapple Paradise Smoothie - Prep Time: 7 minutes ... 13
    10. Nutty Banana Bread Smoothie - Prep Time: 5 minutes 13
    11. Blueberry Basil Bliss Smoothie - Prep Time: 6 minutes 14
    12. Chocolate Mint Marvel Smoothie - Prep Time: 5 minutes 15
    13. Raspberry Lemon Refresher Smoothie - Prep Time: 7 minutes 15
    14. Kiwi Kale Kick Smoothie - Prep Time: 8 minutes 16
    15. Peachy Keen Protein Smoothie - Prep Time: 6 minutes 17
    16. Carrot Cake Comfort Smoothie - Prep Time: 7 minutes 17
    17. Mango Turmeric Tango Smoothie - Prep Time: 6 minutes 18
    18. Vanilla Blue Almond Smoothie - Prep Time: 5 minutes 18
    19. Pineapple Mint Revitalizer Smoothie - Prep Time: 6 minutes .. 19

20. Strawberry Basil Elegance Smoothie - Prep Time: 7 minutes .. 20
21. Cinnamon Pear Serenity Smoothie - Prep Time: 5 minutes 20
22. Blueberry Matcha Zen Smoothie - Prep Time: 8 minutes 21
23. Raspberry Rose Radiance Smoothie - Prep Time: 7 minutes ... 21
24. Mango Ginger Zest Smoothie - Prep Time: 6 minutes 22
25. Chocolate Avocado Dream Smoothie - Prep Time: 7 minutes . 23
26. Kiwi Coconut Symphony Smoothie - Prep Time: 6 minutes 23
27. Blackberry Lavender Tranquility Smoothie - Prep Time: 7 minutes 24
28. Papaya Passion Paradise Smoothie - Prep Time: 8 minutes 24
29. Apricot Almond Euphoria Smoothie - Prep Time: 6 minutes ... 25
30. Cherry Chia Delight Smoothie - Prep Time: 7 minutes 26
CONCLUSION: 27
BONUS: 5 QUICK AND EASY DIABETIC SNACK RECIPES FOR BEGINNERS 29

CONTACT US

We love to interact with our consumers. If you have any questions, observations, or concerns, please contact us by using the email address listed below. We guarantee that all correspondence with us is kept strictly confidential. Thank you!

jammyhealthservice@gmail.com

INTRODUCTION

In a picturesque village, Maria found herself lost and bewildered after being diagnosed with type 2 diabetes. Confusion and desperation clouded her days as she sought a solution to navigate this new chapter in her life.

It was during this tumultuous period that Maria serendipitously stumbled upon the "DIABETIC SMOOTHIE RECIPES BOOK FOR BEGINNERS," a culinary compass that would transform her perception of diabetes management.

This literary treasure, adorned with 30 tantalizing fruit blends, became Maria's beacon of hope. Each page held the promise of a solution to her health concerns, offering not just a guide but a flavorful odyssey that went beyond the ordinary.

The inaugural sip of a mango and kale elixir marked the beginning of a culinary journey that not only pleased her palate but also empowered her to take control of her diabetes.

The book, which started as a lifeline for Maria, soon evolved into a secret shared among a growing community in the village. The confusion that once clouded Maria's path transformed into clarity, and the desperation gave way to a newfound sense of control.

Now, as you stand at the threshold, consider the "DIABETIC SMOOTHIE RECIPES BOOK FOR BEGINNERS" as your guide, unraveling the secret to reclaiming control over diabetes through every flavorful and empowering sip.

Understanding Diabetes:

Diabetes is a chronic condition characterized by elevated blood sugar levels, resulting from insufficient insulin production or the body's inability to use insulin effectively. Insulin is crucial for regulating blood glucose and enabling cells to utilize it for energy.

Types of Diabetes:
Two primary types of diabetes exist. Type 1 diabetes is an autoimmune disorder where the immune system attacks insulin-producing cells. Type 2 diabetes, more prevalent, occurs when the body develops insulin resistance or fails to produce enough.

Causes:
While genetics contribute to Type 1, Type 2 is often linked to lifestyle factors such as poor diet, lack of exercise, and obesity. Age, family history, and certain ethnic backgrounds also increase the risk.

Importance of Diet in Diabetes Management:
Maintaining a healthy diet is vital for managing diabetes. A balanced diet, incorporating controlled carbohydrates, fiber-rich foods, and lean proteins, aids in stabilizing blood sugar levels, managing weight, and reducing complications.

Importance of Smoothies for Diabetes Management:

Carefully crafted smoothies can be a valuable component of a diabetes-friendly diet. By using low-glycemic fruits, leafy greens, and healthy fats, smoothies offer a convenient, tasty way to incorporate essential nutrients.

When portion sizes and ingredients are mindful, smoothies can contribute to stable blood sugar levels, providing individuals with a delicious and nutritious option in their diabetes management plan.

In summary, integrating smoothies into the diet can offer a refreshing and enjoyable approach to meeting the nutritional needs for individuals managing diabetes.

It's crucial to consult healthcare professionals or nutritionists for personalized advice tailored to individual health requirements.

THE 30 EASY AND TASTY RECIPES FOR BEGINNERS

1. Berry Bliss Smoothie - Prep Time: 5 minutes

Ingredients:

1/2 cup blueberries

1/2 cup strawberries

1/4 cup Greek yogurt

1 tablespoon chia seeds

1 cup unsweetened almond milk

Preparation:

Combine blueberries, strawberries, Greek yogurt, chia seeds, and almond milk in a blender. Blend until smooth.

Enjoy the blissful burst of berry flavors!

Importance of Smoothies for Diabetes Management:

Carefully crafted smoothies can be a valuable component of a diabetes-friendly diet. By using low-glycemic fruits, leafy greens, and healthy fats, smoothies offer a convenient, tasty way to incorporate essential nutrients.

When portion sizes and ingredients are mindful, smoothies can contribute to stable blood sugar levels, providing individuals with a delicious and nutritious option in their diabetes management plan.

In summary, integrating smoothies into the diet can offer a refreshing and enjoyable approach to meeting the nutritional needs for individuals managing diabetes.

It's crucial to consult healthcare professionals or nutritionists for personalized advice tailored to individual health requirements.

THE 30 EASY AND TASTY RECIPES FOR BEGINNERS

1. Berry Bliss Smoothie - Prep Time: 5 minutes

Ingredients:

1/2 cup blueberries

1/2 cup strawberries

1/4 cup Greek yogurt

1 tablespoon chia seeds

1 cup unsweetened almond milk

Preparation:

Combine blueberries, strawberries, Greek yogurt, chia seeds, and almond milk in a blender. Blend until smooth.

Enjoy the blissful burst of berry flavors!

2. Green Energy Boost Smoothie - Prep Time: 7 minutes

Ingredients:

1 cup spinach

1/2 cucumber, peeled

1/4 avocado

1/2 cup pineapple chunks

1 tablespoon flaxseeds

1 cup water

Preparation:

In a blender, combine spinach, peeled cucumber, avocado, pineapple chunks, flaxseeds, and water.

Blend until a smooth consistency is achieved.

Feel the energy boost!

3. Citrus Delight Smoothie - Prep Time: 6 minutes

Ingredients:

1 orange, peeled

1/2 cup mango chunks

1/4 cup plain Greek yogurt

1 tablespoon hemp seeds

1 cup coconut water

Preparation:

Peel the orange and combine it with mango chunks, plain Greek yogurt, hemp seeds, and coconut water in a blender.

Blend until smooth. Delight in the refreshing citrus goodness!

4. Almond Joy Smoothie - Prep Time: 5 minutes

Ingredients:

1/4 cup almonds

2 tablespoons unsweetened shredded coconut

1/2 banana

1/2 cup unsweetened almond milk

1 teaspoon cocoa powder

Preparation:

Blend almonds, shredded coconut, banana, almond milk, and cocoa powder in a blender until a creamy texture is achieved.

Indulge in the joy of almonds and coconut!

5. Tropical Paradise Smoothie - Prep Time: 8 minutes

Ingredients:

1/2 cup pineapple

1/2 cup mango

1/4 cup Greek yogurt

1 tablespoon chia seeds

1 cup coconut water

Preparation:

Combine pineapple, mango, Greek yogurt, chia seeds, and coconut water in a blender.

Blend until a tropical paradise flavor is obtained.

Transport yourself to a paradise of tropical delight!

6. Apple Cinnamon Spice Smoothie - Prep Time: 5 minutes

Ingredients:

1 apple, cored and sliced

1/2 teaspoon cinnamon

1/4 cup cottage cheese

1 tablespoon ground flaxseeds

1 cup unsweetened almond milk

Preparation:

In a blender, combine sliced apple, cinnamon, cottage cheese, ground flaxseeds, and almond milk.

Blend until smooth. Savor the comforting taste of apple cinnamon spice!

7. Pomegranate Punch Smoothie - Prep Time: 7 minutes

Ingredients:

1/2 cup pomegranate seeds

1/2 cup mixed berries

1/4 cup plain Greek yogurt

1 tablespoon chia seeds

1 cup water or coconut water

Preparation:

Blend pomegranate seeds, mixed berries, Greek yogurt, chia seeds, and water or coconut water until a refreshing punch is achieved.

Relish the burst of antioxidants!

8. Avocado Berry Burst Smoothie - Prep Time: 6 minutes

Ingredients:

1/4 avocado

1/2 cup mixed berries

1/4 cup cottage cheese

1 tablespoon hemp seeds

1 cup almond milk

Preparation:

Combine avocado, mixed berries, cottage cheese, hemp seeds, and almond milk in a blender.

Blend until a creamy burst of flavors is attained.

Dive into the luscious burst of avocado and berries!

9. Spinach Pineapple Paradise Smoothie - Prep Time: 7 minutes

Ingredients:

1 cup spinach

1/2 cup pineapple chunks

1/4 cup plain Greek yogurt

1 tablespoon chia seeds

1 cup water

Preparation:

In a blender, combine spinach, pineapple chunks, plain Greek yogurt, chia seeds, and water.

Blend until a tropical paradise flavor is achieved.

Bask in the paradise of green and pineapple!

10. Nutty Banana Bread Smoothie - Prep Time: 5 minutes

Ingredients:

1/2 banana

2 tablespoons walnuts

1/4 cup oats

1/2 teaspoon vanilla extract

1 cup unsweetened almond milk

Preparation:

Blend banana, walnuts, oats, vanilla extract, and almond milk in a blender until a smoothie reminiscent of banana bread is attained.

Relish the comforting taste of nutty banana bread!

11. Blueberry Basil Bliss Smoothie – Prep Time: 6 minutes

Ingredients:

1/2 cup blueberries

1/4 cup fresh basil leaves

1/2 cup cucumber, peeled

1 tablespoon chia seeds

1 cup water

Preparation:

Combine blueberries, fresh basil leaves, peeled cucumber, chia seeds, and water in a blender.

Blend until a unique blend of sweet and herby bliss is achieved.

Indulge in the bliss of blueberry and basil!

12. Chocolate Mint Marvel Smoothie - Prep Time: 5 minutes

Ingredients:

1 tablespoon cocoa powder

1/4 teaspoon peppermint extract

1/2 banana

1/4 cup Greek yogurt

1 cup almond milk

Preparation:

Blend cocoa powder, peppermint extract, banana, Greek yogurt, and almond milk in a blender until a refreshing and chocolaty mint marvel is achieved.

Enjoy the marvel of chocolate and mint!

13. Raspberry Lemon Refresher Smoothie - Prep Time: 7 minutes

Ingredients:

1/2 cup raspberries

1/2 lemon, peeled

1/4 cup cottage cheese

1 tablespoon flaxseeds

1 cup water

Preparation:

Blend raspberries, peeled lemon, cottage cheese, flaxseeds, and water in a blender until a zesty and refreshing refresher is achieved.

Sip and feel refreshed with the tantalizing combination of raspberry and lemon!

14. Kiwi Kale Kick Smoothie - Prep Time: 8 minutes

Ingredients:

1 kiwi, peeled and sliced

1 cup kale

1/2 banana

1 tablespoon hemp seeds

1 cup coconut water

Preparation:

Combine peeled and sliced kiwi, kale, banana, hemp seeds, and coconut water. Blend until you feel the invigorating kick of nutrients.

Take a sip and kickstart your day with the powerful blend of kiwi and kale!

15. Peachy Keen Protein Smoothie – Prep Time: 6 minutes

Ingredients:

1/2 cup peaches, sliced

1/4 cup plain Greek yogurt

1/2 cup silken tofu

1 tablespoon chia seeds

1 cup almond milk

Preparation:

Blend sliced peaches, plain Greek yogurt, silken tofu, chia seeds, and almond milk until smooth.

Revel in the protein-packed, peachy delight and let your taste buds dance!

16. Carrot Cake Comfort Smoothie – Prep Time: 7 minutes

Ingredients:

1/2 cup carrots, chopped

2 tablespoons walnuts

1/4 teaspoon cinnamon

1/4 cup cottage cheese

1 cup water

Preparation:

In a blender, combine chopped carrots, walnuts, cinnamon, cottage cheese, and water.

Blend until you experience the comforting taste of carrot cake.

Savor the warmth and comfort with each delightful sip!

17. Mango Turmeric Tango Smoothie - Prep Time: 6 minutes

Ingredients:

1/2 cup mango chunks

1/4 teaspoon turmeric

1/2 banana

1 tablespoon chia seeds

1 cup coconut water

Preparation:

Blend mango chunks, turmeric, banana, chia seeds, and coconut water until you achieve a harmonious tango of flavors.

Take a sip and let the vibrant taste of mango and turmeric dance on your palate!

18. Vanilla Blue Almond Smoothie - Prep Time: 5 minutes

Ingredients:

1/2 cup blueberries

1/4 teaspoon vanilla extract

1/4 cup almonds

1/2 banana

1 cup unsweetened almond milk

Preparation:

Blend blueberries, vanilla extract, almonds, banana, and almond milk until a velvety texture is achieved.

Revel in the sweet and nutty embrace of this vanilla-blueberry delight.

19. Pineapple Mint Revitalizer Smoothie - Prep Time: 6 minutes

Ingredients:

1/2 cup pineapple chunks

1/4 cup fresh mint leaves

1/2 cucumber, peeled

1 tablespoon chia seeds

1 cup coconut water

Preparation:

Combine pineapple chunks, fresh mint leaves, peeled cucumber, chia seeds, and coconut water in a blender.

Blend until you experience the revitalizing essence of pineapple and mint.

Sip and feel refreshed!

20. Strawberry Basil Elegance Smoothie - Prep Time: 7 minutes

Ingredients:

1/2 cup strawberries

1/4 cup fresh basil leaves

1/4 cup Greek yogurt

1 tablespoon flaxseeds

1 cup water

Preparation:

Blend strawberries, fresh basil leaves, Greek yogurt, flaxseeds, and water until an elegantly smooth texture is achieved.

Savor the sophisticated blend of strawberry and basil.

21. Cinnamon Pear Serenity Smoothie - Prep Time: 5 minutes

Ingredients:

1 pear, sliced

1/2 teaspoon cinnamon

1/4 cup cottage cheese

1 tablespoon hemp seeds

1 cup almond milk

Preparation:

In a blender, combine sliced pear, cinnamon, cottage cheese, hemp seeds, and almond milk.

Blend until you feel the serene combination of cinnamon and pear.

Enjoy the comforting serenity in every sip!

22. Blueberry Matcha Zen Smoothie – Prep Time: 8 minutes

Ingredients:

1/2 cup blueberries

1 teaspoon matcha powder

1/4 cup silken tofu

1 tablespoon chia seeds

1 cup almond milk

Preparation:

Blend blueberries, matcha powder, silken tofu, chia seeds, and almond milk until you attain a zen-like harmony.

Take a mindful sip and feel the tranquility with every sip!

23. Raspberry Rose Radiance Smoothie – Prep Time: 7 minutes

Ingredients:

1/2 cup raspberries

1 teaspoon rose water

1/4 cup plain Greek yogurt

1 tablespoon flaxseeds

1 cup water

Preparation:

Blend raspberries, rose water, plain Greek yogurt, flaxseeds, and water until a radiant texture is achieved.

Sip and embrace the radiant blend of raspberry and rose water.

24. Mango Ginger Zest Smoothie - Prep Time: 6 minutes

Ingredients:

1/2 cup mango chunks

1/2 teaspoon grated ginger

1/2 banana

1 tablespoon chia seeds

1 cup coconut water

Preparation:

Combine mango chunks, grated ginger, banana, chia seeds, and coconut water in a blender. Blend until you feel the zesty zest of mango and ginger. Take a sip and experience the invigorating zest!

25. Chocolate Avocado Dream Smoothie - Prep Time: 7 minutes

Ingredients:

1/4 avocado

1 tablespoon cocoa powder

1/2 banana

1/4 cup silken tofu

1 cup almond milk

Preparation:

Blend avocado, cocoa powder, banana, silken tofu, and almond milk until a dreamy texture is achieved.

Savor the indulgent dream of chocolate and avocado with every sip!

26. Kiwi Coconut Symphony Smoothie - Prep Time: 6 minutes

Ingredients:

1 kiwi, peeled and sliced

1/4 cup shredded coconut

1/2 cup cucumber, peeled

1 tablespoon hemp seeds

1 cup coconut water

Preparation:

Combine peeled and sliced kiwi, shredded coconut, peeled cucumber, hemp seeds, and coconut water.

Blend until you experience the symphony of kiwi and coconut.

Enjoy the tropical symphony in a glass!

27. Blackberry Lavender Tranquility Smoothie - Prep Time: 7 minutes

Ingredients:

1/2 cup blackberries

1/4 teaspoon dried lavender buds

1/4 cup plain Greek yogurt

1 tablespoon flaxseeds

1 cup water

Preparation:

Blend blackberries, dried lavender buds, plain Greek yogurt, flaxseeds, and water until a tranquil texture is achieved. Immerse yourself in the calming blend of blackberry and lavender.

Take a sip and experience the tranquility!

28. Papaya Passion Paradise Smoothie - Prep Time: 8 minutes

Ingredients:

1/2 cup papaya chunks

1/4 cup passion fruit pulp

1/4 cup silken tofu

1 tablespoon chia seeds

1 cup coconut water

Preparation:

Combine papaya chunks, passion fruit pulp, silken tofu, chia seeds, and coconut water in a blender.

Blend until you feel the passion in every sip.

Indulge in the paradise of papaya and passion fruit!

29. Apricot Almond Euphoria Smoothie - Prep Time: 6 minutes

Ingredients:

1/2 cup apricots, sliced

1/4 cup almonds

1/2 banana

1 tablespoon hemp seeds

1 cup almond milk

Preparation:

In a blender, combine sliced apricots, almonds, banana, hemp seeds, and almond milk.

Blend until you attain a euphoric texture.

Sip and immerse yourself in the euphoria of apricot and almonds!

30. Cherry Chia Delight Smoothie – Prep Time: 7 minutes

Ingredients:

1/2 cup cherries, pitted

1 tablespoon chia seeds

1/4 cup plain Greek yogurt

1/2 cup cucumber, peeled

1 cup water

Preparation:

Blend pitted cherries, chia seeds, plain Greek yogurt, peeled cucumber, and water until a delightful texture is achieved.

Delight in the cherry goodness and chia crunch.

Take a sip and experience the delightful blend of cherry and chia!

These 30 diabetic-friendly smoothie recipes offer a symphony of flavors, each crafted to enhance your well-being while managing diabetes. Incorporate these tantalizing creations into your routine, and embark on a journey of delightful sips that contribute to your overall health.

Cheers to a vibrant and delicious way of managing diabetes! Enjoy every sip, and embrace the goodness of a health-conscious lifestyle!

CONCLUSION:

Dear Valued Reader,

As you reach the end of " Diabetic Smoothie Recipes Book for Beginners: The Comprehensive Guide for the Newly Diagnosed to Take Control of Diabetes and Lower Blood Sugar Levels With 30 Easy and Tasty Fruit Blends," we want to express our sincere appreciation for your trust in this transformative journey. Your health is our priority, and we care deeply about your well-being.

Navigating the challenges of a diabetes diagnosis can be overwhelming, and we applaud your commitment to taking control of your health. The story of Maria and the carefully crafted smoothie recipes shared in this book are not just words on pages; they are a testament to the power of making mindful choices for a healthier life.

Remember, you are not alone on this journey. We value you and your health, and we are here to support you every step of the way. If you have questions, need guidance, or simply want to share your progress, feel free to reach out to us at jammyhealthservice@gmail.com.

Your journey matters, and we are committed to helping you thrive.

As a special bonus, we've included snack recipes to add even more variety to your diabetes-friendly culinary adventures. These snacks are our gift to you, a small token of appreciation for your dedication to a healthier lifestyle.

To continue your exploration of valuable resources, scan the QR code below for access to more value-packed books from us. Each piece is designed with your well-being in mind, providing insights, recipes, and strategies to empower you on your health journey.

SCAN TO GAIN ACCESS TO MORE BOOKS FROM ME

May your path be filled with vitality, resilience, and joy. Here's to your health and the wonderful journey ahead. We wish you well and we eagerly await your response.

Happy Sipping....

With heartfelt wishes,

Michael Jammy

jammyhealthservice@gmail.com

BONUS: 5 QUICK AND EASY DIABETIC SNACK RECIPES FOR BEGINNERS

1. Greek Yogurt Parfait - Prep Time: 5 minutes

Ingredients:

1 cup Greek yogurt (unsweetened)

1/2 cup fresh berries (blueberries, strawberries, or raspberries)

1 tablespoon chopped nuts (almonds or walnuts)

1 teaspoon honey (optional for sweetness)

Preparation:

Layer Greek yogurt with fresh berries in a bowl or glass.

Top with chopped nuts for added crunch and a drizzle of honey if desired.

Enjoy this protein-packed and fiber-rich parfait.

2. Veggie Sticks with Hummus - Prep Time: 10 minutes

Ingredients:

Assorted vegetable sticks (carrots, cucumber, bell peppers)

1/4 cup hummus (store-bought or homemade)

Preparation:

Wash and cut the vegetables into sticks.

Serve with hummus for a satisfying and nutritious snack.

Hummus provides protein and healthy fats, while veggies add vitamins and fiber.

3. Avocado and Tomato Salsa - Prep Time: 7 minutes

Ingredients:

1 ripe avocado, diced

1/2 cup cherry tomatoes, halved

1/4 cup red onion, finely chopped

Fresh cilantro, chopped

Salt and pepper to taste

Preparation:

In a bowl, combine diced avocado, cherry tomatoes, chopped red onion, and cilantro.

Season with salt and pepper to taste.

Serve with whole-grain crackers for a delicious and heart-healthy snack.

4. Baked Cinnamon Apple Chips - Prep Time: 15 minutes

Ingredients:

2 apples, thinly sliced

1 teaspoon cinnamon

1 tablespoon olive oil

Preparation:

Preheat the oven to 225°F (107°C).

In a bowl, toss apple slices with cinnamon and olive oil until evenly coated.

Line a baking sheet with parchment paper and place the slices on it.

Bake for 1.5 to 2 hours until the apples are crisp.

Enjoy these sweet and crunchy apple chips without added sugars.

5. Quinoa and Vegetable Salad - Prep Time: 20 minutes

Ingredients:

1/2 cup cooked quinoa (cooled)

1/2 cup cherry tomatoes, halved

1/4 cup cucumber, diced

1/4 cup feta cheese, crumbled (optional)

Fresh lemon juice and olive oil for dressing

Preparation:

In a bowl, combine cooked quinoa, cherry tomatoes, cucumber, and feta cheese.

Drizzle with fresh lemon juice and olive oil for a light and refreshing dressing.

Toss the ingredients together and enjoy a nutrient-rich and satisfying salad.

These snack recipes not only provide nutritional benefits but also come together quickly for your convenience. For personalized dietary advice, always consult with a healthcare professional or a licensed dietitian.

...WISHING YOU THE BEST...

Made in the USA
Columbia, SC
18 July 2025

Made in the USA
Columbia, SC
18 July 2025